W9-BSD-678

Toward Genocide

David Downing

WORLD ALMANAC® LIBRARY

Please visit our web site at: www.worldalmanaclibrary.com
For a free color catalog describing World Almanac® Library's list of
high-quality books and multimedia programs, call 1-800-848-2928 (USA)
or 1-800-387-3178 (Canada). World Almanac® Library's fax: (414) 332-3567.

Library of Congress Cataloging-in-Publication Data

Downing, David, 1946-
    Toward genocide / by David Downing.
        p. cm. — (World Almanac Library of the Holocaust)
    Includes bibliographical references and index.
    ISBN 0-8368-5945-6 (lib. bdg.)
    ISBN 0-8368-5952-9 (softcover)
    1. Holocaust, Jewish (1939-1945)—Juvenile literature. 2. Genocide—Europe—
History—20th century—Juvenile literature. I. Title. II. Series.
D804.34.D683   2005
940.53'18—dc22   2005040779

First published in 2006 by
World Almanac® Library
A Member of the WRC Media Family of Companies
330 West Olive Street, Suite 100
Milwaukee, WI 53212 USA

Copyright © 2006 by World Almanac® Library.

Produced by Discovery Books
Editors: Geoff Barker, Sabrina Crewe, and Jacqueline Gorman
Designer and page production: Sabine Beaupré
Photo researchers: Geoff Barker and Rachel Tisdale
Maps: Stefan Chabluk
Consultant: Ronald M. Smelser, Professor of Modern German History, University of Utah
World Almanac® Library editorial direction: Mark J. Sachner
World Almanac® Library editor: Alan Wachtel
World Almanac® Library art direction: Tammy West
World Almanac® Library production: Jessica Morris

Photo credits: cover: USHMM, courtesy of Zydowski Instytut Historyczny Instytut Naukowo-Badawczy; title page: USHMM, courtesy of Charles and Hana Bruml; p. 5: USHMM, courtesy of Library of Congress; p. 6: Topfoto.co.uk; p. 7: Mary Evans Picture Library/Weimar Archive; p. 11: Mary Evans Picture Library; p. 12: Mary Evans Picture Library/Weimar Archive; p. 15: Three Lions/Getty Images; p. 16: USHMM, courtesy of B. Ashley Grimes II; p. 18: CORBIS; p. 21: David Chaim Ratner/USHMM, courtesy of Eliezer Zilberis: p. 23: Topfoto.co.uk; p. 25: USHMM, courtesy of Zydowski Instytut Historyczny Instytut Naukowo-Badawczy; p. 27: Time Life Pictures/Getty Images; p. 28: USHMM, courtesy of Gedenkstätte Buchenwald; p. 31: USHMM, courtesy of Shlomo (Solly) Perel; p. 35: Carl Strott/USHMM, courtesy of Zentrale Stelle der Landesjustizverwaltungen; p. 36: Friedrich Franz Bauer/USHMM, courtesy of James Blevins; p. 38: Topfoto.co.uk; p. 39: ARCFI Group; p. 41: Topfoto.co.uk; p. 43: Topfoto.co.uk.

Printed in Canada

1 2 3 4 5 6 7 8 9 09 08 07 06 05

Cover: This photo shows inhabitants of the Jewish Warsaw Ghetto, Poland, walking past the corpses of fellow Jews—victims of hunger and disease.

Title page: Nazis made Jews wear a Star of David on their clothes to show that they were Jewish. *Jude* is the German word for Jew.

Contents

The Holocaust

The Murder of Millions

The word *holocaust* has a long history. In early times, it meant a burnt offering to the gods, and in the **Middle Ages**, a huge sacrifice or destruction. It still has this second meaning today, particularly when used to describe large-scale destruction by fire or nuclear weapons. But since the 1970s, the word has gained a new and specific meaning. Today, when people refer to the Holocaust—with a capital "H"—they mean the murder of approximately six million Jews by Nazi Germany and its **allies** during World War II.

This crime had deep historical roots. In predominantly Christian Europe, the Jews had always been considered a race apart and had often endured persecution for that reason. When governments or peoples wanted someone to blame for misfortune, they often picked on an innocent and helpless, Jewish minority.

In the early twentieth century, many Germans wanted some-one to blame for their defeat in World War I and the terrible economic hardship that followed. They, too, picked on the Jews in their midst—with ultimately horrific results. The Holocaust was ordered and organized by political leaders, carried out by thousands of their willing supporters, and allowed to happen by millions of ordinary people.

The scale of the crime is still hard to take in. To use a modern comparison, about three thousand people were killed in the **terrorist** attacks in the United States on September 11, 2001. Between June 1941 and March 1945, an average of four thousand European Jews were murdered every day.

These people were killed in a variety of ways. Some were left to starve, some to freeze. Many were worked to death in **labor camps**. More than one million were shot and buried in mass graves. Several million were gassed to death in specially built **extermination camps** such as Auschwitz and Treblinka.

The Persecution of Jews

Jews were not the only victims of the Nazis. In fact, it is probable that the Nazis and their allies murdered at least five million other **civilians** before and during World War II. Their victims were killed for a variety of reasons: **communists** for their political opinions, **homosexuals** for their sexual orientation, people with mental disabilities for their supposed uselessness to society, **Gypsies** and Slavs for their supposed racial inferiority, and Russians, Poles, and other eastern Europeans because they happened to be in the Nazis' way.

The central crime in the Holocaust—the murder of millions of Jews—was a long time in the making. Most of the actual killing took place between 1941 and 1945, but the Jews of Germany were subject to intense persecution from the moment Adolf Hitler and his Nazi Party took power in 1933. That persecution was itself merely the latest in a series of persecutions stretching back over almost two thousand years, in which every nation of Europe had at some time played a part.

This book looks at the time between the outbreak of World War II in September 1939 and the building of the **death camps** in 1941 and 1942—the period of the Nazi transition to **genocide**.

A Ukrainian Jew is shot by a German soldier at the edge of a pit already filled with corpses.

CHAPTER ONE

Europe at Their Mercy

Conquests

War broke out in Europe on September 1, 1939, when Germany invaded Poland. Germany had signed a **non-aggression treaty** with the Soviet Union (the Nazi-Soviet Pact) only one week earlier, so they expected no problems or objections from the Soviets. They also hoped that Britain and France, which had promised earlier in 1939 to come to Poland's aid if Germany invaded, would simply protest and do nothing. In this, the Germans were disappointed. The British and French took no actual military steps to help Poland, but they did declare war on Germany and refused to accept anything less than a complete German withdrawal from Poland as the price of peace. Germany did not withdraw, and Poland fell within a month.

A single German soldier drives captive civilians down a Polish country road in September 1939.

German motorized troops drive through a bombed-out Polish village in September 1939.

The next six months—from early October 1939 to early April 1940—are called the "phony war" because nothing much seemed to happen. There were occasional naval and air battles, but the great powers, though officially at war with each other, made no attempt to attack with their armies. Then, in early April 1940, the Germans struck, occupying both Denmark and Norway in a lightning campaign. In May 1940, they invaded the Netherlands, Belgium, Luxembourg, and France. They conquered the first three countries in just a few days and drove the French—and the British forces supporting them—back north toward Paris and the coast of the English Channel. By mid-June, British forces had retreated across the English Channel, and the French had surrendered.

Hitler waited, hoping that the British would now accept a compromise peace. When the British refused, he began gathering a fleet to carry his armies across the English Channel. Before such a fleet could sail and Hitler could invade by sea, however, the Germans needed control of the skies. Their attempt to win this during the summer of 1940—the weeks of aerial duels and bombings that are known as the Battle of Britain—ended in failure for Germany.

Even with that defeat, however, by the autumn of 1940, Hitler and the Nazis had achieved a position of complete

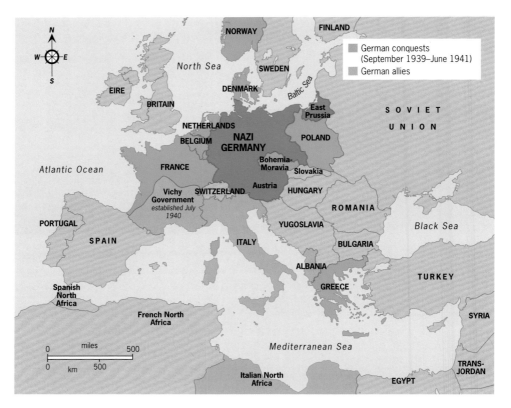

This map of Europe shows Germany's conquests from September 1939 to June 1941. Germany had made Austria part of its nation in 1938.

dominance in continental Europe. From the English Channel to the borders of the Soviet Union, from the Mediterranean Sea to the Arctic Circle, there was no one left to mount an effective challenge to them. All the nations within that area were occupied by Germany, friendly to Germany, or too weak to resist any German demands.

Occupations

By the autumn of 1940, German troops were occupying all, or a substantial part, of eight countries—Czechoslovakia, Poland, Denmark, Norway, the Netherlands, Luxembourg, Belgium, and France. The Nazi government had shown little sign of respecting generally accepted principles of human rights and justice in its own country during the prewar years, and it showed next to none in the countries it now occupied.

There were, however, big variations in the way German troops and other forces—the police, civil administrators, and the **SS** (the elite Nazi force, also known as the blackshirts)— treated the populations of the different occupied countries. At one extreme, from the very first day of the invasion, German actions in Poland showed a complete disregard for internationally accepted rules of behavior in both war and occupation. Captured soldiers were frequently denied their rights as prisoners of war and were often simply executed. Civilians were not treated any better. Huge amounts of property and goods

The Fate of Poland

After it was defeated by Germany in September 1939, Poland was divided between Germany and the Soviet Union. The German half was then divided again: The northern and western regions were annexed by the **Third Reich** (or simply the Reich, as the German regime was called), while the southeastern area became a German colony, the so-called General Government.

Those areas annexed by the Reich were slowly "Germanized"; Poles were expelled, and Germans were brought in to take over their homes and land. The General Government, which included the major cities of Warsaw, Krakow, and Lublin, became a virtual slave state. Many thousands of professional and middle-class Poles and thousands of Catholic priests were murdered with the intention of turning the Polish nation into a leaderless working class. According to Heinrich Himmler, the leader of the SS, the people of such a state would need little education—they would only be taught simple arithmetic ("up to 500 at most"), how to write their own name, and obedience to the Germans. Himmler considered it "unnecessary to teach reading."

were simply seized, and large numbers of civilians were forced to leave the homes that their families had occupied for centuries. People were randomly murdered on the streets. No attempt was made to protect the weak and helpless from the consequences of war. Indeed, many attempts were made to increase their suffering.

At the other extreme, the occupation of Denmark was a comparatively polite affair and caused little more than inconvenience to most Danes. The most important reason for the difference lay in the different positions that Poles and Danes occupied in the Nazis' racial **hierarchy**. The Danes were considered fellow "**Aryans**" (members of Hitler's so-called master race), while the Poles—non-Jewish Poles, that is—were considered only slightly superior to Russians, Jews, and animals. Most of the other peoples in occupied countries found themselves somewhere between these two extremes. They were not

"Aryans"

The Nazis believed that all the races of the world had a natural position in a hierarchy of human worth. In their view, the "Aryan" race—the name was taken from a group of languages—included Germans and Scandinavians and was supposedly superior to all the others. The English and Dutch came just below them, the French and Italians further down, the Slavs of eastern Europe further down still. The Jews were considered the lowest of the low, even an evil "anti-race." The Nazis also believed that history was a continuing struggle between races. They thought that the "Aryans," with their natural supremacy, had the right and duty to win this struggle but that there was always the chance they would be defeated by superior numbers or underhanded trickery.

This photo shows a group of expelled Slovak Jews on their way to the Hungarian border in 1939. Following the German occupation of Hungary in 1944, some or all of these men would have been sent to their deaths at Auschwitz.

as blessed as Germans, and they were not as cursed as Poles, Slavs, and Jews.

During this period, countries including Italy, Slovakia, Hungary, Romania, Bulgaria, and Yugoslavia remained independent in name, but their governments knew they could not afford to antagonize the Germans. Some—like the government of newly independent Slovakia—were only too happy to copy the **anti-Semitic** behavior of the Nazis, while others—such as the governments of Hungary and Germany's ally Italy— only introduced anti-Semitic **legislation** reluctantly. All were eventually forced into line. If there was one thing that Nazi Germany expected of neighboring nations, it was that they punish Jews just for being Jews.

CHAPTER TWO

The Plight of the Jews

Nazi Intentions

In the summer of 1940, there were about 4 million Jews living
in Germany itself and those countries occupied by the German
army in the previous two years. Roughly three-fourths of them
(about 3 million) lived in Poland. Another 1.5 million Jews
lived in European countries allied to Germany or subject to
its wishes, and a further 2.5 million lived in the western Soviet
Union (in the European part of Russia, Ukraine, Lithuania, and

This 1930s cartoon from a Nazi schoolbook, *Trust No Fox on the Heath
and No Jew on His Word*, shows a procession of cruelly caricatured
Jews leaving Germany. Non-Jewish children happily look on.

Latvia). In 1940, the Nazi government held the power of life or death over the 4 million Jews living in Germany or its occupied territory, and it had considerable influence over the fate of the other millions of Jews. What exactly were its intentions?

Over the centuries, extreme anti-Semitism toward the Jews of Europe had been expressed in four main ways: through **forced conversion**, **segregation**, **expulsion**, and murder. Since the Nazis saw Jews as a race and not simply a religious group, there was no point in trying conversion. Racial segregation and expulsion had both been tried during the 1930s, but neither was successful in solving the Nazi's "Jewish problem." In addition, Nazis actually took pleasure in persecuting Jews— they could neither leave them alone nor allow them an easy departure. Besides, **emigration** of the Jews to locations beyond Europe had been stopped by the outbreak of war. And by 1940, the Reich had also assumed responsibility for the Jews of Poland. If the Nazis could not find a way to segregate or expel these 3 million Jews, then—given their anti-Semitic goals— murder would be their only remaining option.

Making a Lie Come True

"I do not understand how this kind of people is biologically capable of remaining alive. Every morning a large contingent of laborers of younger Jews, aged between twenty and thirty, passes by our platoon: Each one of them looks from their eyes with galloping **consumption**. Figures that can elsewhere only be seen in hospitals walk around by thousands. . . . Added to the biological corruption is the filth, which cannot be described."

*The diary entry of a German soldier in Poland for November 11, 1939, showing the success of six years of Nazi anti-Semitic **propaganda**. The unsanitary conditions in which Poland's Jews now lived—mostly the result of German ill-treatment, as well as of the Jews' treatment in prewar Poland—were now being used to back up Nazi claims that Jews were naturally unclean and disease-ridden.*

What Was Possible?

Through 1940 and the first half of 1941, the Nazi leadership tried to come up with a clear policy toward the Jews. From their point of view, this was not an easy task. They might simply wish to destroy the Jews, but would such a policy make political or military sense? Until the war was won, Jews might prove useful in several ways. German industry needed workers as more and more men were called into the military, and Jews could be made to work for virtually nothing. In addition, the mere threat of killing the Jews might be used to keep the United States from entering the war.

Even if these arguments were ignored, was the outright murder of millions of people a realistic proposition? Would the German people be prepared to carry it out? Was it even possible to kill that many Jews with the weapons and technology that were available? And could they get away with it? There

Jud Suess

The movie *Jud Suess* (*The Jew Suess*) premiered in Berlin in September 1940. Based on a novel intended by its author to expose anti-Semitism, the movie twisted the original story to suit its own, anti-Semitic purposes. It tells of an eighteenth-century Jew named Suess Oppenheimer who cheats his way up from the **ghetto** to become chief minister to the Duke of Würtemberg. He then shamelessly manipulates the upright duke in pursuit of money and power and ends up raping the duke's daughter. The daughter can remove this racial shame only by committing suicide. The hate-filled movie, which featured two of Germany's most famous actors, was shown throughout the Reich and occupied Europe. Such "popular entertainments" were important carriers of the message that the Nazis sought to spread across Europe.

were few clear answers
to these questions, and
the policies of the Nazi
leadership in this period
reflected that lack of
clarity. The four contra-
dictory urges of Nazi
policy toward the Jews—
to hurt them, use them,
expel them, and kill
them—were all given
free rein, but the empha-
sis given to each impulse
varied widely from place
to place.

In Poland and Elsewhere

In Poland, a reign of
terror descended on the
country's three million
Jews. During the first
fifty-five days of the
occupation (during
September and October
of 1939), more than five
thousand Jews were
executed by the German
invaders—for the simple
"crime" of being Jewish.
Individuals suffered fatal

**A young Jewish man sells yellow
armbands bearing the Star of David
on the streets of Warsaw in the early
months of 1940. The wearing of such
armbands became compulsory for
Polish Jews about this time.**

beatings, groups were executed in mass hangings, and at least
two **synagogues** were set on fire with their congregations
locked inside. After this period, there were fewer such acts of
random violence, but the plight of the Polish Jews continued to
worsen. A torrent of new laws removed all their political and
economic rights, and hundreds of thousands were forced into

German soldiers stand guard on a street in Czestochowa, Poland, in September 1939. The corpses of Jewish men they have shot lie on the ground in front of the buildings.

separated sections—or ghettos—of the major towns and cities. There, in conditions of severe overcrowding and terrible poverty, they were required to work for the Germans until the Nazi leadership reached a final decision about their future.

In the other countries occupied by German forces in 1939 and 1940, the plight of the Jews seemed, for the moment, less serious. They were increasingly subject to different laws restricting their rights to move and work, but there was no attempt in western Europe to imprison them in camps or ghettos.

A Territorial Solution?

At this stage, the Nazi leadership was still considering alternatives to genocide. For one thing, Jews were still being allowed to emigrate from Germany until the autumn of 1941. For another, the Nazis were still obsessed with the idea of finding a suitable spot on the planet for the Jews to live. Several options were suggested. The area around Lublin, in that part of occupied Poland called the General Government, was the first choice. This had the advantages, from the Nazi point of view, of being both available and extremely poverty-stricken. Unfortunately, it had bigger disadvantages: It was too small and too close to Germany.

During the summer of 1940, the idea of moving the Jews to distant Madagascar—a large, French-owned island in the Indian Ocean with an African population of about four million—gained popularity in Nazi circles. The scheme collapsed because of the Nazi failure to defeat Britain. As long as the British navy controlled the Atlantic and Indian Oceans, there was no way of transporting millions of Jews to Madagascar.

The search for a place to dump the Jews—a **reservation** rather than a homeland—went on. As 1940 gave way to 1941 and conflict with the Soviet Union grew nearer (despite the non-aggression treaty), Nazi thoughts turned increasingly in the direction of the Soviet Union. Somewhere out there, they told themselves, somewhere in the vastness of "the East," they would find the territorial solution to their "Jewish problem."

In the Polish Town of Sieradz

"I saw German soldiers dragging Jewish men from their houses, and kicking and beating them in the street; with horror I noticed that my father was among them. The Jewish men were forced to run towards the market place, whereupon two rows of armed German soldiers were waiting for them. They then had to run through the German gauntlet where they were savagely kicked and clubbed with rifle butts. My cousin, Idle Natal, only twenty-one years old, was kicked to death in this melee."

*Arek Hersh, eleven-year-old Polish Jew in the early years
of World War II, Sieradz, Poland*

CHAPTER THREE

In the Ghetto

The Creation of the Ghettos

Between September 1939, when World War II began, and 1942, the Nazis created Jewish ghettos in more than 100 Polish, Lithuanian, Latvian, and Russian towns. (Germany invaded the Soviet Union in June 1941.) The small Polish town of Piotrkow was the site of the first ghetto in September 1939. The two largest were established in Lodz and Warsaw, Poland, in February 1940 and October 1940 respectively. About 0.5 million Jews were crowded into the Warsaw Ghetto and a further 160,000 into the one at Lodz.

In most cases when a ghetto was established, there was a period of transition, lasting several weeks, in which the ghetto remained "open." During this period, Jewish residents could come and go, but once the ghettos were declared "closed," the

Children help spray and brush the streets of the Warsaw Ghetto with chlorine in 1941. Residents fought a constant battle against the disease epidemics caused by terrible living conditions.

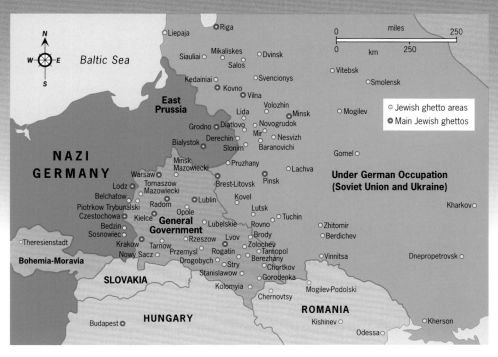

This map shows the main Jewish ghettos in Europe in 1941–1942.

residents became prisoners. High walls topped with barbed wire surrounded the larger ghettos. No attempt was made to provide the Jews in each ghetto with a fair division of the facilities and space they had once shared in the city with non-Jews. On the contrary, every attempt was made to give the Jews as little space as possible and to make their lives as miserable as possible. In Warsaw, for example, where Jews made up one-third of the city's population, they were given only a few square miles and 2 percent of the city's housing, which meant an average of seven people to each room. Running water and electricity were always in short supply, and the Jewish hospital was deliberately situated outside the ghetto walls. The ghettos were clearly intended not just to isolate the Jews but as a form of punishment.

Cut off from the outside world, Warsaw's Jews were almost completely reliant on their jailers for work and food—food that often was not given. More than fifty thousand inhabitants of the Warsaw Ghetto starved to death in the twenty months that followed its establishment.

Running the Ghettos

Given such conditions, it seems surprising that many Jews welcomed the establishment of the ghettos. One reason was that the ghettos seemed, at first, to offer some sort of **sanctuary**. German soldiers and officials did enter the ghettos, often with evil in mind, but on a day-to-day level, the Jews were generally left on their own. Although the conditions were awful, most residents could still live with their families. They might be in a prison, but they still had some freedom inside it. Moreover, on that same day-to-day level, the business of local administation was still handled by their own people.

In each ghetto, the Germans chose a Jewish council, or *Judenrat*, to administer the ghetto's daily affairs. Each council was responsible for the supervision of health care, education, food distribution, justice, burials, culture, and industry in its ghetto. When the Germans demanded workers for the labor camps, it was these councils that chose who would go. This suited the Germans, of course. The Jewish councils did the Nazis' dirty work for them, and council members were often blamed by their fellow Jews for doing precisely that.

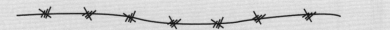

Hunger in the Ghetto

"Two little boys are begging in the street next to our gate. I see them every time I go out. Or they might be girls, I don't know. Their heads are shaven, clothes in rags, frightfully emaciated tiny faces bring to mind birds rather than human beings. Their huge black eyes, though, are human; so full of sadness. . . . The younger one may be five or six, the older ten perhaps. They don't move, they don't speak. The little one sits on the pavement, the bigger one just stands there with his claw of a hand stretched out."

Warsaw Ghetto resident Janina Bauman,
diary entry dated April 18, 1941

Small numbers of ghetto children were able to study in hiding. These children had secret lessons in a stable in the Kovno Ghetto in Lithuania. Lithuania was then part of the German-occupied Soviet Union.

Trying to Survive

For most ordinary Jews, life in the Nazi-created ghettos was a nonstop struggle simply to survive. There was never enough food. There was rarely enough room to sleep. In the winter, it was impossible to keep warm. Killer diseases such as **typhus** and **tuberculosis** (TB) were widespread.

Even if the Germans had left the Jews to fend for themselves, the residents' chances of survival would have been poor. As it was, the Germans actively worked at turning the lives of ghetto dwellers into a living nightmare. There were random visits by drunken soldiers, and snipers came who took pleasure in picking off inhabitants from vantage points beyond ghetto walls. Germans harassed Jews by arresting them for breaking unknown rules, and there was always the threat of being chosen for work in the world outside. As the months went by, that world became more of a mystery to those in the ghettos. They had no radios, no phones, and no reliable mail delivery. Rumors circulated that increasingly filled people with horror.

Yet despite all the misery and fear, and the endless difficulties of day-to-day existence, ghetto life was not completely bleak. Education was forbidden by the Nazis, but children were taught in secret. Jewish religious and cultural life continued regardless of Nazi efforts to suppress it. Jewish residents produced their own musical concerts and plays, wrote their own poems, and created their own art. In most ghettos, at least one person kept a record of what was happening.

Life went on, and hope persisted. When the Germans were eventually defeated, the Jews told each other, then everything could be put back the way it had been. It was true that their hopes of the British and French defeating the Germans had come to nothing, but there were still hopes of the Americans, of the Russians. When news of the Germans' June 1941 invasion of the Soviet Union reached the Polish ghettos, there was a feeling of celebration. With the enormous resources of the Soviet Union now deployed against Hitler, the Jews believed a German defeat could not be too far away.

The Dilemma of *Judenrat* Members

By creating the Jewish councils, the Nazis hoped to save themselves the trouble of running the ghettos as well as to turn Jew against Jew. The Jews knew this, but there was little that those chosen to serve on a council (*Judenrat*) could do. Refusing to serve would probably result in their execution and merely mean that someone else would have to make the same choices. The council decided who got the jobs inside the ghetto—jobs that often meant the difference between starvation and survival. It decided which of their people would be sent to labor camps, and it sometimes tried to persuade the Germans to take more of their people. Council members did this hoping that the more indispensable their ghetto became, the less chance there was of it being closed down altogether. As the war went on, council members knew they were sending people to die. After the war, some people claimed the council members had been little better than **collaborators**, that without them the Nazis would have found it much harder to organize the Holocaust. Most historians, though, stress the utterly impossible position in which the Jewish councils found themselves.

German troops interrogate inhabitants of the Warsaw Ghetto during the mass deportations to the death camps in 1942.

Rumors of Worse

It was not to be. All through that summer of 1941, the news was of German military advances and Soviet military defeats. More and more young Jews were taken away from the ghettos to work in labor-starved factories of the Reich. In November, the Nazis began selecting increasing numbers of ghetto Jews for "resettlement" in the East. At first, the Jewish councils tried to convince themselves and their people that this was the long-promised territorial solution, that the Nazis had finally found a place to send them. But rumors of mass murder began filtering back, and the councils changed their tactics, encouraging their people to work harder and harder. They wanted to make their particular ghetto indispensable to the Nazi war effort and to postpone for as long as possible the day when they would be "resettled." They tried to prevent their ghetto from being closed down, its families divided and sent away to unknown destinations and fates.

Through the winter of 1941–1942, the deportations went on, no one ever returned, and terrible rumors circulated. By the spring of 1942, each ghetto, each Jewish council, each Jew, knew that no matter how hard they worked, or how indispensable they tried to become, they were all marked down for murder.

CHAPTER FOUR

The Camps

Camps of Many Kinds

Between the outbreak of war in 1939 and the summer of 1941, a large number of Europe's Jews—and an even greater number of non-Jews—found themselves more or less permanently imprisoned in different camps. There had been camps in Germany since 1933. Between then and 1939, they had been filled with **socialist**, communist, and Christian enemies of the Nazis and those whom the Nazis called "a-socials"—alcoholics, homosexuals, Gypsies, criminals, and prostitutes, among others. Many of these inmates were also Jewish, and they were usually treated worse because of it. However, with the exception of the weeks following *Kristallnacht* in November 1938, few Jews were imprisoned just for being Jewish. These peacetime camps were called **concentration camps**, and many of them—like Dachau, for example (the first concentration camp, located in southern Germany)—survived in this role right through the war. During the war years, however, other types of camps were also built, often in huge numbers. Throughout Nazi-occupied Europe, the Nazis and their local allies built camps for prisoners of war, camps for imprisoning local enemies, and **transit camps** for gathering people (principally Jews) whom they wanted to ship elsewhere. Wherever slave workers were needed, they built labor camps. In Poland, for example, more than eighty-five labor camps had been set up by the end of 1939.

Where manufacturing was involved, the labor camps housed both the laborers and their workshops; where outdoor work was involved, the camps simply provided barracks for the workforce. Some labor camps were more temporary than others. When, for example, a marsh had been drained or a fortification completed, the camp set up for that purpose was no longer needed. It would be broken up and its workers moved elsewhere.

A guard beats a prisoner at Poniatowa labor camp in Lublin, Poland. Jewish prisoners were forced to work in sewing workshops and on road construction. There were mass executions inside and outside the labor camp.

Some of the men, women, and children who ended up in these wartime camps had said or done something that the Germans considered hostile, but most had simply found themselves in the wrong place at the wrong time. In complete violation of all international agreements covering prisoners of war, captured soldiers were routinely put to work in such camps. Once the war had begun, any Jew could be sent to a labor camp just for being Jewish. In Poland, the Germans simply seized able-bodied Jewish youths on the streets until the Jewish councils agreed to supply the number of workers needed.

Conditions in the Camps

Most concentration camps and labor camps were run by the SS. The one thing all the camps had in common was a terrifying indifference to the well-being of their inmates. The conditions were almost indescribably bad. As in the ghettos, there was never enough food or warmth. There was family and religious life in the ghettos, however, as well as some highly limited freedoms, to provide some compensation for all the misery and hardship. In the camps, there was little of this, only endless roll calls to attend, rules to obey, orders to follow, and long hours of often backbreaking work. The inmates did what they were told, but even obedience was rarely enough. A momentary failure to look sufficiently grateful could invite a beating, and such beatings often ended in death.

In the early years of the Nazi regime, it was claimed that the main job of the concentration camps was to "reeducate" inmates, to show them the truth of Nazi ideas. From the

The SS

The SS (*Schutzstaffel,* or defense unit) began as a unit of the **SA** (the Nazis' private army), detailed to act as Hitler's personal bodyguard in 1925. Heinrich Himmler became leader of the SS in 1929 and slowly built it into the Nazi Party's combined private army, police force, and security service. The SS split off from the SA to become an independent group and adopted black uniforms, earning their name of "blackshirts." SS members were fiercely loyal to Hitler and his ideas and were supposedly drawn only from pure Aryan stock. After 1933, the organization split into three groups: general units, concentration camp guard units, and armed units that eventually fought alongside the regular army. In 1939, the concentration camp guard units and armed units merged as the *Waffen*-SS. By the height of the war, the SS was using its control of the camps to run a vast array of businesses producing everything from soft drinks to its members' own uniforms. During the 1930s, the SS also took control of Nazi Germany's police and security services. In 1939, Himmler's deputy, Reinhard Heydrich, was appointed head of the new RSHA (Main Office for Reich Security), which controlled the operations of the **Gestapo** (political police), *Kripo* (criminal police), and *Sicherheitsdienst* (or **SD**, the Nazi Party intelligence and security service).

Nazis push Jewish ghetto inhabitants into line outside a Polish railroad station. They would next be moved to labor camps or to the gas chambers of one of the extermination camps.

beginning, this "reeducation" involved a great deal of physical abuse, but most political opponents were eventually released. Once the war began, the abuse increased, and releases grew less frequent. The Nazis now had two, often contradictory, aims. The old wish to hurt and punish was counterbalanced by a new, desperate, war-driven desire to get as much work as was humanly possible out of their captive labor force.

In normal times and societies, the owners and managers of businesses have a vested interest in keeping their workers well-fed, well-housed, and well-rewarded. Such employees, after all, tend to work harder and more efficiently. Even a slave owner on a Southern plantation in the United States before the Civil War had a vested interest in keeping his or her slaves alive—they were, after all, not worth anything to the owner if they were dead. The Nazis, faced with a seemingly endless supply of "subhuman" slave labor, saw no reason not to work each individual to death. "*Vernichtung durch Arbeit*"—"destruction through work"—was the German phrase for this. Not surprisingly, most labor camps had their own crematoriums for burning the dead.

Prisoners from the Buchenwald concentration camp in Germany are forced to take part in building the Weimar-Buchenwald railroad in 1943.

Medical Experiments

There was one other specific use to which the camps were put: as centers of medical experimentation. In most concentration camps, doctors used inmates as laboratory animals, measuring their responses to changes in external conditions and to new foods, new treatments, and new drugs. Some prisoners, for example, were kept in refrigerated conditions until they got frostbite, so that a variety of possible cures could be tried on them. The more successful cures could then be used to help German soldiers who were suffering through the harshness of winter while fighting in the Soviet Union. The intense suffering endured during these experiments, and the death of many

Camp Rules

Rules that were established at the Dachau concentration camp were later extended throughout the camp system. The following are some extracts:

1. Punishments allowed at any time: beatings, drilling (repeated physical exercises), no mail or food, tying to stakes.

2. Three days' solitary confinement for anyone who does not keep his bed or room in proper order or takes a second helping of food without permission.

3. Five days' solitary confinement for anyone who sits or lies on his bed during the day without permission.

4. Eight days' solitary confinement (and a whipping of twenty-five strokes before and after) for anyone who makes ironical remarks about an SS officer or who does not show respect. . . .

5. The following will be hanged: Anyone who, at any point, discusses politics; forms a political group; loiters with others; collects true or false information about the concentration camps . . . ; tries, by climbing onto barrack roofs or up trees, to contact the outside world with signals, lights, or so on; tries to escape, commit a crime, or persuade anyone else to do so; attacks a guard or SS man; refuses to obey an order, encourages mutiny; leaves a marching column or place of work; shouts, agitates or makes speeches on the march or at work.

of those who were experimented on, was not considered important. As far as the Nazis were concerned, inmates could just as well die in a camp's medical unit as from overwork in the camp itself or from hunger and disease in the ghettos. In the spring of 1941, the death camps had not yet been built, but the Jews were already dying in huge numbers.

CHAPTER FIVE

Operation Barbarossa

The Invasion

On June 22, 1941, the German armed forces invaded the Soviet Union. Hitler's long-term aim, as outlined almost twenty years earlier in his autobiography and statement of political intentions *Mein Kampf,* had always included the destruction of the Soviet Union (which he saw as the joint creation of international Jewry and international communism). He had another goal: to build a new German empire in the vast "living space" that would then become available.

Things went well for Germany during the opening months of the invasion, which had been named Operation Barbarossa after a medieval German emperor. Hundreds of thousands of

This map shows German advances during the war in the East until the end of 1941.

Adolf Hitler (center left) visits a unit of the 12th German Panzer Division during the first summer of the war in the Soviet Union.

Soviet prisoners were taken, and by the end of September 1941, the German forces were more than two-thirds of the way to Moscow. Stiffening Soviet resistance, however, and an unusually early winter slowed and eventually stopped the German advance. By December 1941, all hopes of an easy victory for the Germans had vanished.

Leaving the Rulebook Behind

Military histories of the Barbarossa campaign tend to concentrate on strategy and tactics, because they were what most affected its outcome. However, for the people involved—both military and civilian—the most important thing about Operation Barbarossa was the way it was conducted, without mercy or any respect for internationally accepted rules governing behavior in time of war. This decision to defy the rules was taken by Hitler and enthusiastically endorsed by his fellow Nazis in both the SS and the armed forces. When they were fighting people whom they considered racial equals or near-equals in western Europe and North Africa, German soldiers behaved reasonably well. When they were invading a country full of people whom their leaders considered subhuman—Slavs and Jews—many German soldiers completely lost touch with their own humanity.

The savageness of the Nazi onslaught in the Soviet Union was planned from the beginning. In both March and June 1941, the army and SS met to discuss rules of conduct in the forthcoming campaign, and the army agreed that the SS would be given a free hand in the areas behind the front line. Field-Marshal Walther von Reichenau later issued an Order of the Day to his troops, saying that they "must show full understanding of the necessity of the severe but just **atonement** being required of the Jewish subhumans."

The *Einsatzgruppen*

Who was to administer this "atonement"? In June 1941, four SS "action units," known as ***Einsatzgruppen***, moved into the Soviet Union behind the four major army groups. Their written orders, as issued by Himmler's deputy Reinhard Heydrich on July 9, were to execute all communist officials, all Jews who worked for the Communist Party or state, and any other "extremist elements." Anti-Jewish feeling among the Soviet population was to be "secretly encouraged."

The *Einsatzgruppen* were also, according to one witness, given a verbal order to kill all or any Jews whom they came across. Whether or not such a specific order was given, the three thousand men of the *Einsatzgruppen* were fully aware that their leaders considered it both acceptable and desirable to murder any Jews. Moreover, there is no evidence that they

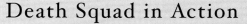

Death Squad in Action

"The people who had got off the lorries [trucks] had to undress on the orders of an SS man who was carrying a whip in his hand. They had to place their clothing on separate piles for shoes, clothing and underwear. Without weeping or crying out these people undressed and stood together in family groups, embracing each other and saying good-bye while waiting for a sign from another SS man who stood on the edge of the ditch and also had a whip.

"I watched a family, a man and woman both about fifty years old with their children of one, eight and ten, as well as two grown-up daughters of about twenty and twenty-four. The father held the ten-year-old boy by the hand speaking softly to him. The boy was struggling to hold back tears. The father pointed a finger to the sky and stroked his head and seemed to be explaining something to him.

"At this moment the SS man near the ditch called out something to his comrade. The latter counted off some twenty people and ordered them behind the mound. The family of which I have just spoken was among them.

"I walked round the mound and stood in front of the huge grave. The bodies were lying so tightly packed together that only their heads showed, from almost all of which blood ran down over their shoulders. Some were still moving. The ditch was already three-quarters full. I estimate that it already held a thousand bodies.

"I turned my eyes towards the man doing the shooting. He was an SS man; he sat, legs swinging, on the edge of the ditch. He had an automatic rifle on his knees and he was smoking a cigarette."

Hermann Gräbe, German construction worker,
giving evidence about Operation Barbarossa
at the postwar Nuremberg Trials, November 1945

tried, in practice, to make any distinction between Jews who worked for party and state and those who did not.

As the army advanced into parts of the Soviet Union (Russia, Byelorussia, Ukraine, and the Baltic states), the *Einsatzgruppen* scoured the conquered towns and villages for communists and Jews. They received considerable help from anti-Semitic locals, many of whom started killing Jews before the *Einsatzgruppen* arrived. Most of the Soviet communist officials had fled eastward, but a high proportion of the Jews— well over 1 million—were caught by the speed of the German advance. The same procedure was followed in each town and village: Once a convenient hole in the ground had been found or dug by a few prisoners, Jews were assembled, taken in batches (with the men first) to the killing area, stripped of their clothes and any remaining possessions, lined up on the edge of the hole, and shot. The numbers and times involved varied wildly. The few Jews of a tiny village could be killed in a matter of minutes, while the 10,000 Jews of Kishinev were murdered in fourteen days of relentless slaughter. The most infamous massacre took place at a ravine called Babi Yar, just outside Kiev. Here, according to the meticulous records of the *Einsatzgruppen* responsible, 33,771 Jews were shot dead, each layer of bodies covered by sand before the next was added. Many of the victims, wounded but not killed by the bullets, were buried alive. In the first five weeks of Operation Barbarossa, more Jews were killed than in the previous eight years of Nazi rule. By Christmas 1941, the *Einsatzgruppen* had shot about 0.5 million Jewish men, women, and children.

When Was the Decision for Genocide Made?

While these mass shootings were taking place in the Soviet Union, other Jews were being forced into new ghettos. German industry's need for slave workers remained as compelling as ever. At this point, several Nazi leaders talked of a "final solu- tion" to the "Jewish problem," but the meaning of this phrase seemed to change from person to person, month to month. In early 1941, for example, it was clearly being used to describe

Nine Jewish women stand at the edge of a mass grave in Liepaja, Latvia, on December 15, 1941. They await execution by a firing squad of Latvian and German police officers. In just three days, 2,700 Jews were murdered at this location.

the creation of a Jewish reservation in some distant part of the Soviet Union.

So when did Hitler and the Nazis finally decide on genocide? There is no written record of such an order being given, and it seems unlikely that the precise date will ever be known. Most historians agree that only Hitler—who always disliked leaving written records—could have given the order, and that he gave it orally at some point in the second half of 1941. Various events have been taken as evidence of the intent to commit genocide— for example, Reinhard Heydrich's July 9 order to the *Einsatzgruppen* to kill Jews; a speech by Nazi official Hermann Göring about the "final solution to the Jewish problem" on July 31; the first transport of western European Jews to the East in October—but none offers conclusive proof that the decision to commit genocide had been made.

Heinrich Himmler chats with a German soldier in July 1941. By this time, he controlled the police, intelligence, and political administration in occupied territories and the concentration camp system in Poland.

How?

More significant, perhaps, were the growing signs that the murder of millions was becoming easier to accomplish. In the summer of 1941, Himmler, the SS leader, went to observe a mass execution outside Minsk. He was seriously shocked—not by the fact of mass murder, but by the terrible **psychological** strain the shootings were putting on the murderers. A less stressful method of killing large numbers of people was needed. A solution to this problem was already at hand. Since 1939, about seventy thousand people with mental disabilities had been murdered in specially constructed gas chambers and vans as part of the **T-4 euthanasia program**. In the Nazis' eyes, there seemed no reason why the same methods should not be used to kill Jews. In September 1941, an extremely effective gas named Zyklon B (hydrogen cyanide) was successfully tested on Soviet prisoners of war at the Auschwitz concentration camp in southern Poland. Himmler noted with satisfaction that "the unpleasantnesses connected with shooting are removed." The question of "how?" had been solved.

Why?

Why did the Nazis deliberately set out to kill every Jew in Europe? It was partly because they had run out of other options in their struggles for racial supremacy and to rid Germany of a Jewish presence. It was partly because now they could. For Hitler and the other Nazi leaders, the decision,

The First Gassings

The practice of euthanasia—of putting to death people with incurable diseases or conditions—was supported by many Germans, particularly the Nazis, from the early 1920s. The cost of keeping these people in homes was one reason given for this support, while another was the idea that they represented a "weak strain" in the German race. When the Nazis came to power in Germany in 1933, they began by ordering the **sterilization** of such people so that the "weak strain" would not be passed on to another generation.

In 1935, Hitler decided that, in the event of war, the nation would no longer be able to afford to keep all its sick and disabled people alive, and that mentally and physically disabled people would be put mercifully to death. In September 1939, the first month of the war, a euthanasia program was put into effect. Those running the program visited institutions all over Germany to select their victims, and, by August 1941, some seventy thousand people had been killed. The murders were mostly carried out in newly built gas chambers at euthanasia centers, but in northeastern Germany, mobile gas vans were used. It was these vans that were used at Chelmno death camp in Poland in the fall of 1941 for the first mass gassings of Jews.

The gas chamber at Mauthausen concentration camp in Austria. Mauthausen was not a death camp as such, and this chamber was relatively small, holding only 120 people at most. Nevertheless, about 10,000 people were murdered in this room between 1942 and 1945.

at last, to embark on a thorough campaign of genocide was probably a great relief. They hated the Jews with a fierceness that today's world might find hard to understand, but which seemed completely reasonable to them and to many others in Europe. Hitler was a monster, but a monster who believed he was doing the world a service.

If killing Jews was such a horrific thing to do, Hitler might have asked, then why were the Ukrainians, the Lithuanians, the Slovaks, and the Romanians all so happy to help? Why was the Vichy regime in France (the puppet government established by the Nazis after the German occupation of France) so eager to get rid of its own Jews? Anti-Semitism was common in France, as it was in many other European countries. And genocide, after all, was nothing new. The Turks had done their best to wipe out the Armenians twenty-five years before, and—as Hitler was fond of remembering—had not been called to account.

For Hitler, in late 1941, it was not so much a question of "why?" as "why not?" The technology was there, and the SS was eager to get started with building and running extermination camps. The army, further brutalized by its war in the East,

Chelmno Death Camp

"The newcomers were . . . told . . . that they were going to work in the East, and promised . . . fair treatment and good food . . . [but] first they must take a bath and deliver their clothes to be disinfected. From the courtyard they were sent inside the house, to a heated room on the first floor, where they undressed. They then came downstairs to a corridor, on the walls of which were inscriptions: "to the doctor" or "to the bath"; the latter with an arrow pointing to the front door. When they had gone out they were told that they were going in a closed van to the bath-house.

"Before the door of the country house stood a large lorry [truck] with a door in the rear, so placed that it could be entered directly with the help of a ladder. . . . When the whole of one batch had been forced in [to the van], the door was banged and the engine started, poisoning with its exhaust those who were locked inside. The process was usually complete in four or five minutes, and then the van was driven to [a] wood about 4 kilometers [2.5 miles] away, where the corpses were unloaded and burnt."

Taken from a Polish official postwar report by
Judge Wladyslaw Bednarz, 1946

would look the other way. The need for laborers in the factories remained, but the gas chambers couldn't kill all the Jews at once. There would be sufficient slave labor for quite a while.

CHAPTER SIX

The Wannsee Conference

Planning Murder

On January 20, 1942, a conference was called by Himmler's deputy, Reinhard Heydrich, in the leafy Berlin suburb of Wannsee. Those invited included representatives of the German administrations in occupied Poland and the Soviet Union, SS and Nazi Party officials, and representatives from government ministries involved in dealing with Jewish affairs. The Wannsee Conference was not called to decide the fate of Europe's Jews— the decision to murder them had already been made in 1941. The Wannsee Conference took place to clarify matters; to coordinate the work of the many agencies that would be involved in carrying out the killing; to ensure the supremacy of the SS in the operation; and to answer any minor questions that remained.

The need for clarification was obvious. Jews were already being killed in huge numbers, but no clear instruction had been passed down to all those involved in carrying out the Nazi policies. As one Nazi administrator in the occupied territories had asked the SS in November 1941, was the killing of the Jews to take place "without regard to age and sex and their usefulness to the economy?" He had no objection to killing Jews—he just wanted clear instructions from above.

These instructions were provided by Heydrich at Wannsee. Put simply, those Jews considered unfit for work would be killed, and those who could work would be worked to death. Only the strongest would survive, and they would be killed before they could form the "germ cell of a new Jewish revival." The most important of the minor questions remaining concerned the fate of half-Jews, quarter-Jews, and Jews married to non-Jews. It was agreed at Wannsee that almost everyone with any Jewish blood would be killed. A few exceptions would be sterilized.

The representatives of the various ministries and administrations were sent away to organize and coordinate this program of extermination. Throughout Europe, Jews had to be rounded up and detained until trains were available. Timetables had to be devised, because the trainloads of Jews bound for extermination camps had to share space on the rails with the armed forces. The camps and their gas chambers had to be built.

Reinhard Heydrich (1904–1942)

Reinhard Heydrich joined the Nazis in 1931 after being discharged from the German navy for dishonorable conduct. He was introduced to Heinrich Himmler, who admired Heydrich's organizational ability, ruthlessness, and extreme anti-Semitism and who gave him the job of leading the Nazi Party's own security service, the SD. Heydrich went on to head the RSHA (Main Office for Reich Security), which controlled all Gestapo police and intelligence forces, and to organize the murderous *Einsatzgruppen* in Poland and the Soviet Union. Ordered by Göring in the summer of 1941 to come up with a realistic "final solution to the Jewish problem," Heydrich supervised the use of mobile gas vans at Chelmno and organized the Wannsee Conference in January 1942. Four months later, he was assassinated in Prague, Czechoslovakia, by a group of Czech soldiers.

Into the Holocaust

In January 1942, Britain and the Soviet Union remained unde-feated, and the United States had recently entered the war (after the Japanese attack on Pearl Harbor, Hawaii, the month before). As 1942 unfolded, however, both Germany and its ally Japan enjoyed a string of victories. The Japanese briefly threat-ened Hawaii and Alaska. Meanwhile, the German army pushed Soviet forces back toward Stalingrad and the oil-rich Caucasus region, and British forces in North Africa back toward the Nile River. In the summer of 1942, therefore, victory still seemed within Hitler's grasp.

It was against this background that the Nazi persecution of the Jews shifted from an orgy of often arbitrary killing to a systematic program of genocide. Of the six camps known as death camps, only Chelmno, with its gas vans, was already

Spelling out Genocide

"In the course of the Final Solution and under appropriate leadership, the Jews should be put to work in the east. In large, single-sex labor columns, Jews fit to work will work their way eastwards constructing roads. Doubtless the large majority will be eliminated by natural causes. Any final remnant that survives will doubtless consist of the most resistant elements. They will have to be dealt with appropriately, because otherwise, by natural selection [the survival of the fittest], they would form the germ-cell of a new Jewish revival.

"In the course of the practical execution of the Final Solution, Europe will be combed through from west to east . . . The evacu-ated Jews will be first sent, in stages, to so-called transit ghettos, from where they will be transported to the east."

From the minutes of the Wannsee Conference,
Berlin, January 1942

The ramp at Birkenau (Auschwitz II) is shown above in 1944. These newly arrived Hungarian Jews have been divided into those who are fit to work and those—children, some women, and the elderly—who are not. Those considered unfit to work would be marched straight from the ramp to the nearby gas chambers.

operating at the time of the Wannsee Conference. Like Chelmno, the other five were built in occupied Poland, three of them from scratch. These three—Belzec, Sobibor, and Treblinka—began operation in March, April, and July 1942, respectively. Extermination facilities at the already existing concentration camps of Auschwitz and Majdanek were ready by May and November of the same year.

As the German armed forces undertook their last vain surge for victory, trains of overcrowded cattle cars began rolling from ghettos and transit camps all over Europe toward the new killing grounds of occupied Poland.

Time Line

1933 Nazis gain power in Germany. First concentration camp opens at Dachau.

1938 November 9: *Kristallnacht* in Germany: Thousands of Jewish shops and synagogues are burned and destroyed, about 100 Jews are killed and 30,000 arrested (1,000 of those arrested are later killed in captivity).

1939 August: Nazi-Soviet Pact is reached between Adolf Hitler and Joseph Stalin.
September 1: German attack on Poland begins World War II.
September: Polish defeat is followed by German reign of terror; first Jewish ghetto in Poland is created at Piotrkow.
Euthanasia program murders begin in Germany.
October: "Phoney war" between Germany and Allies begins.
First of many labor camps is set up in Poland.

1940 February: Lodz Ghetto is established.
April: "Phoney war" ends with German invasions of Denmark and Norway.
May: Germany attacks Belgium, the Netherlands, Luxembourg, and France.
June: France surrenders to Germany. Vichy France is established in southeastern France.
September: Germany loses the Battle of Britain.
October: Warsaw Ghetto is established.

1941 March: German army and the SS discuss treatment of civilians in the forthcoming war against the Soviet Union.
June 22: Germany invades the Soviet Union in Operation Barbarossa.
July 9: Reinhard Heydrich issues order for the killing in the Soviet Union of all captured communists and Jews employed by the state; mass shootings of Soviet Jews by *Einsatzgruppen* occurs.
July 31: Hermann Göring talks of a "final solution to the Jewish problem" in a speech.
September: Zyklon B gas is tested on Soviet prisoners of war at Auschwitz concentration camp.
October: First transport of western European Jews to the East.
Fall: Gas vans begin regular operations at Chelmno death camp in Poland.
December 7: Japanese attack on Pearl Harbor brings the United States into the war.

1942: January 20: Wannsee Conference is held in Berlin to finalize plans for Jewish genocide.
March–November: Five more death camps in Poland begin mass extermination operations.

Glossary

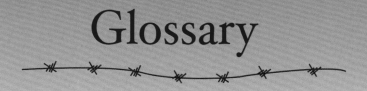

allies: people, groups, or nations that agree to support and defend each other. "The Allies" were the nations that fought together against Germany in World War I and World War II.

anti-Semitic: expressing prejudice against Jews.

Aryan: according to the Nazis, a superior section of the white race, often distinguished by blue eyes and blond hair.

atonement: making amends for a wrongdoing.

civilian: person who is not serving in the armed forces.

collaborator: person who actively assists the foreign occupiers of his or her country.

communist: person who believes in the principles of communism, a political system in which the government owns and runs the nation's economy. (A Communist with a capital "C" is a member of the Communist Party.)

concentration camp: prison camp set up by the Nazis to hold Jews and other victims of the Nazi regime. Many prisoners held in these camps were never tried or given a date of release.

consumption: tuberculosis of the lungs, a life-threatening disease.

death camp: another term for extermination camp.

Einsatzgruppen: special SS units operating behind the advancing German army and ordered to murder Jews and other enemies of the Nazis.

emigration: leaving of a country of residence to go and live somewhere else.

expulsion: forcible removal or banishment.

extermination camp: place set up by Nazis in which they murdered large numbers of people.

forced conversion: forcing someone to adopt a different religion.

genocide: deliberate murder or attempted murder of a whole people.

Gestapo: political police force of the Nazis.

ghetto: usually poor and overcrowded part of a city, occupied by a minority group because of social, legal, or economic pressure.

Gypsy: member of a group that includes the Roma and Sinti peoples, who live mostly in Europe. Gypsies are traditionally nomadic, meaning they move from place to place.

hierarchy: grading or ranking of individuals.

homosexual: person attracted to others of the same sex.

Kripo: criminal police department of the Nazis.

Kristallnacht: (Night of Broken Glass), a Nazi attack in November 1938 on Jews and Jewish property.

labor camp: camp in which prisoners are forced to perform hard labor.

legislation: law or body of laws.

Middle Ages: period of European history from about A.D. 500 to 1500.

non-aggression treaty: agreement not to behave in an aggressive manner.

propaganda: promotion and spreading of ideas, often involving either a selective version of the truth or plain lies.

psychological: having to do with or influencing the mind.

reservation: area of land on which a particular group of people are confined or sent to live.

SA: short for *Sturmabteilung*, the Nazi private army also known as "the brownshirts."

sanctuary: place of refuge and safety.

SD: short for *Sicherheitsdienst*, the Nazi intelligence and security service.

segregation: separation of one group of people from another in order to set up barriers between them.

socialist: person who believes in socialism, a set of ideas which emphasizes the needs of the community as a whole rather than the freedoms or needs of the individual.

SS: short for *Schutzstaffel*, a Nazi elite force also known as "the blackshirts."

sterilization: practice of making people unable to have children.

synagogue: Jewish place of worship.

T-4 euthanasia program: Nazi program that undertook deliberate killing of people with supposedly incurable conditions or diseases.

terrorist: person who performs acts of violence in order to make a political point or force a change in government policy.

Third Reich: name given by the Nazis to their regime. The name means "third empire," following the First Reich (the medieval Holy Roman Empire) and the Second Reich (1870–1918).

transit camp: camp where people are kept prior to being moved elsewhere.

tuberculosis: infectious, life-threatening disease causing fever and wasting and often affecting the lungs.

typhus: infectious, life-threatening disease characterized by high fever and rashes.

Further Resources

Books

Altman, Linda Jacobs. *The Holocaust Ghettos* (Holocaust Remembered). Enslow Publishers, 1998.

Byers, Ann. *The Holocaust Camps* (Holocaust Remembered). Enslow Publishers, 1998.

Saldinger, Anne Grenn. *Life in a Nazi Concentration Camp* (The Way People Live). Lucent Books, 2000.

Sherrow, Victoria. *The Blaze Engulfs: January 1939 to December 1941* (Holocaust). Blackbirch Press, 1998.

Shuter, Jane. *Life and Death in Hitler's Europe* (The Holocaust). Heinemann Library, 2003.

Web Sites

The Holocaust: Crimes, Heroes and Villains
www.auschwitz.dk
Web site about those involved in the Holocaust, with biographies, poetry, photos, and more.

The Holocaust History Project
www.holocaust-history.org
Archive of documents, photos, and essays on various aspects of the Holocaust.

Holocaust Survivors
www.holocaustsurvivors.org
Interviews, photos, and sound recordings of survivors of the Holocaust.

The Museum of Tolerance's Multimedia Learning Site
motlc.wiesenthal.org
Educational Web site of the Simon Wiesenthal Center, a Jewish human rights agency.

Non-Jewish Holocaust Victims
www.holocaustforgotten.com
A site dedicated to the Nazis' five million non-Jewish victims.

United States Holocaust Memorial Museum
www.ushmm.org
Personal histories, photo archives, and museum exhibits of the Holocaust.

About the Author

David Downing has been writing books for adults and children about political, military, and cultural history for thirty years. He lives in Britain.

Index